T0194713

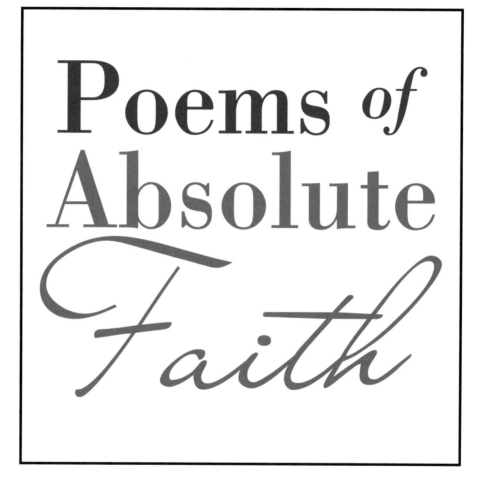

Poems of Absolute *Faith*

LYNN SIMPSON

AuthorHouse™
1663 Liberty Drive
Bloomington, IN 47403
www.authorhouse.com
Phone: 833-262-8899

Because of the dynamic nature of the Internet, any web addresses or links contained in this book may have changed since publication and may no longer be valid. The views expressed in this work are solely those of the author and do not necessarily reflect the views of the publisher, and the publisher hereby disclaims any responsibility for them.

Any people depicted in stock imagery provided by Getty Images are models, and such images are being used for illustrative purposes only.
Certain stock imagery © Getty Images.

This book is printed on acid-free paper.

Library of Congress Control Number: 2022911570
ISBN: 978-1-6655-6313-0 (sc)
ISBN: 978-1-6655-6314-7 (e)

Print information available on the last page.

Published by AuthorHouse 07/07/2022

authorHOUSE®

Contents

Call Him

Call Him up anytime.
It costs less than a dime.

Call on Him to release what's on your mind.
He'll respond in a manner sweet, gentle, and kind.

He's waiting to bless
And deliver you from this mess.

Lying is not His nature.
Too late—here comes the rapture.

He loves all children,
Just like a mother hen.

He is the great divine.
I'm His, and He is mine.

As the blessings keep flowing,
His love keeps growing.

God's Riches at Christ's Expense: Jesus Came to Set Us Free

Grace is all I need.
He is all I want to
Love with all my mind.
And he will keep his promises
To love your generation eternally.
Jesus came to set you free.
Do not worry about a thing.
A long time ago he died
To give us victory on this side,
In everything we do and say.
Today, he wants to give you a hug.
As I worship and adore his church,
The most wonderful name in all the earth.
He is the greatest of the great.
I am, I am his beloved child.
He came for you and me.
Fed for today, though tomorrow is far away.
Love him now and receive a crown.

He is always there for you and me,
Giving out of his treasure.
'Cause his love is everlasting,
There is peace of mind for all his children.
His mercy endures through every generation,
And nothing can ever bring a separation.
I am weak, yet he is strong.
Give him all you have today.
He will open the door and show you the way.
Lovingly, he will play seek and find.
Today, all is yours, only believe
That he came and died for sins.
In the end, everybody wins.
Shower peace, and release the beast.
He is always watching over his children
To keep us from harm.
He is the lover of my very soul today.
His precepts are the only way.

Seed of Faith, Let It Grow

Purer than the driven snow,
Digest the Word so the spirit will grow.

Each branch shall lengthen
As his church is strengthened.

Gloria fe cam us te.

Friend or foe ever.
Each day drawing us nearer.

Loveliest friend is not a has-been.
Faithful and true till the very end.

Love, Peace, and Grace

He loves me
All the time.
I know He is mine.

He is here,
So very near.
Listen, my dear.

Peace, I know.
Love apparently shows.
Grace has to grow.

Read His will.
Paid all the bills.
Is free still.

Reach for Him today.
Truth is the only way.
Only believe this is your day.

Under His Wing

Listen carefully
To the instructions that be.

The quicker the obedience,
The sweeter the deliverance.

I am able to fix the least.
I will move you to a greater peace.

Were you ever in the field,
Under My wing and shield?

I will perform great acts before thee now.
Glory hallelujah, what a beautiful crown!

Embrace His Comeliness

Longing for His embrace
Is so much better than the race.

He is the only man who understands.
Truly He has a majestic plan.

For He has picked me up
To drink from a bitter cup.

Not my will but Thine alone
Is all there is in this world of dry bones.

He came to deliver the letter to man
And blessed the nation that is more than sand.

The Olive Leaf

He is my olive leaf
From the receding flood.

You are my hope for the days to come.
With all my heart, I will praise you now.

Of this branch I will become thine,
Together forever, a part of the divine.

Chasten me with the rod
For understanding is precious to thee.

In thy sight is fullness of joy,
Oh, leaf brought forth to witness of thee.

Stallion and All

I believe that I have the greatest Father
As his Son arose in my life.
Content in all stages of tribulation
Is to know all his victories.
Evaluate the circumstance,
And see Jesus in the midst.
Listen to his prompt.
Step into the boat of obedience.
Press through into the heavenlies
Although you are in over your head.
Demonic illusions
To cloud the solution.
At last he is here,
Stallion and all,
Just for the cause.

His Return

Jesus is coming again.
He's making a way to return.

This is one appointment you want to make.
Don't let Satan make you late.

Jesus is coming soon,
With or without a moon.

Don't let your eyes get hooked
On the things of this world.
But pray for each man, woman, boy, and girl.

Jesus is comin' back,
And he's not going to see if you're red, yellow, black, or white.

Just like Noah and the flood,
He used his precious blood
To purify our souls, to make us whole.

Jesus is on the way now.
What a beautiful light and sound.

Will he meet us in the street
Or visit us while we sleep?

Seek Him First

Hear him, hear him loud and clear.
This is your year, my dear.

Cleanse your ears 'cause here comes the new world.
It is the greatest thing I've ever heard.

Seek him first is all you need to do now.
With his return, he'll give you a crown.

Open your heart, and let him come in.
Salvation is now; don't wait till the end.

To give him your soul is all that is required.
Stay focused on him, and faith will bring about desires.

First things first, for better or worse.
Just make sure you don't arrive in a hearse.

The Faithful Servant

There's no place I'd rather be

Than in His presence daily (continually)

For God has done such amazing things.

Ah, how I wish that I could sing

His praises night and day.

Count up the costs and hear Him say,

"Well done, My faithful servant.

The righteous receive the covenant.

Well done, well done, you made it through."

Oh, how I longed for this day to begin,

To gather each one under my wing.

Depart, depart ye worker of iniquities.

The glorious kingdom is not for thee.

Rain from heaven, fire, brimstone, and the like

For justice is served, sweet dreams, good night.

Meditate on the Love

Thank You for taking the pain away

As far as the east is from the west each day.

Reach for Him as close as your next breath.

On the journey, make a choice before death.

Love Him now, while it is fresh in your mind.

Submit to His call; pick a place and a time.

Forgetting the mess is truly for the best.

Meditate on the love, and enter into His rest.

Turn away from the evil path today,

And follow the yellow brick highway.

Plant Love

Who are you searching for

What are hoping for?

Let it be, let it be.

Let it be, let it be.

Have everything you need?

Help your neighbor to plant a seed.

Let it grow, let it grow.

Let it grow, let it grow.

And the Master will nourish

The little ones that He cherishes.

God is all day, all month, all year.

God who changes not as the seasons.

Grace Divine

Up, up, and away, my beautiful swan.
Grace is your gift divine.

Knock, knock on the door of my heart.
Please carve out a statue so grand.

Sing, sing aloud, my little red robin
For music is natural to thee.

Crow, crow early in the morning, the rooster three,
Before the end draws near.

Hold on Tight

Somebody's praying over here, Lord.

Somebody's crying over here, my Savior.

Somebody's fasting for direction.

They're worshipping and seeking Your face.

Though the winds do blow

Or there are ten inches of snow,

Hold on, and never stop reaching for the moon.

Jesus will be arriving soon, yes very soon.

Keep kneeling and believing.

The power of His Word is healing.

Yes, God is restoring your soul.

Trust in Him to make you whole.

He is the one I spend time with daily,

A true gentleman with respect for a lady.

People may come with deception;

Never give in to temptation.

Continue to obey His every command.

Revelation to distinguish a boy from a man.

The victory is won.

Behold what He has done.

Telegram

Help, Lord.

Help, Lord.

Help, Lord, today.

Send deliverance.

Send deliverance.

Send deliverance right away.

Jesus, Jesus.

Jesus, Jesus.

Jesus, Jesus, we pray.

Return here.

Return here.

Return here right now.

Reveal the root.

Reveal the root.

Reveal the root somehow.

Destroy them.

Destroy them.

Destroy them; this is your will.

Peace, Lord.

Peace, Lord.

Peace, peace be still.

Chronicles 3

Clocking in, checking out.
Taking care of this, looking over that.

Lying about this, scheming over that.
Can barely see the truth.

How can you teach the youth?
Heard about it, read through it

Search around town.
Shop at the boutique.
Suspicious about him, concerned about her.

We will surely see the light
When Jesus comes to fight.

His Pleasures Forevermore

Awake to Your presence is all that I long.

To receive a fresh anointing and to worship in song.

For in Him is comfort unmeasured.

Mighty Thy hand behold all treasure.

Donate, I pray, my organs for a king

That the seed may continue to spring.

Neither water nor food can fill the spirit man.

Yes, I leaped straight into His hand.

True gifts need not a box or a bow,

Yet a willing vessel washed white as snow.

Peace of love sewn in each boy and girl,

The Father revealed in a chaotic world.

Covered in Love

Thank you, Lord, for planting

The Tree of Life that's right

For my family without strife.

Allowing me to see graciously

All the mysteries that be

By all the powers that operate in thee.

It is your pleasure

To let down your good treasure.

For your will

Is to pay the bill.

Gracias, I'm the patient.

The Greatest

You're the greatest healer,
Though the sting seems realer.

Covered in love we're able to live.
Time is winding down.

There's just too much in the cup.
Peace be still,

It is the Father's will.

Strong in the Lord

(Psalm 107:24–25)

Strong in His love.

Strong in His grace.

Strong in His blood.

Strong in His dove.

Strong in His Word.

Strong in His herd.

Strong in His ways.

Strong in His days.

Strong in His laws.

Strong in His cause.

Strong in His peace.

Strong in His lease.

Strong in His arms.

Strong in His palms.

Strong in His wind.

Strong in His end.

Great Works:
He Needs No One At All

Fat, skinny, short, or tall,

He's mighty in all His works.

He's great in all the worlds.

This is His Son's perfect love.

Anything great is from above.

Each of us is indispensable.

His mercy fully incomprehensible.

Seek Him with praying and fasting.

While your time is lasting,

Have not you noticed His touch,

Or how He loves you so much?

I serve a mighty God

Who works to set us free.

To deliver your wretched soul

From a blazing heap of coals.

Once Crucified for Me

On the day pride raises its head,

Lord, crucify me.

On the day condemnation intervenes,

Father, justify me.

When nobody knows my name,

Meet Jesus, the One who can change everything.

Have you had a bitter day?

Come to Jesus any minute of the hour.

He will show you the perfect way.

As you love Him more,

That is when you will testify

Of how they stretched my Lord

To the tree and crucified Him to death.

In the Master's Hand

All caught up in the cares of this world,
Burden so heavy as an Egyptian pharaoh.
But I kept calling on my Savior,
Pleading for one small favor.
And when my hope ran out, I felt
His Spirit begin to shout.
Because He returned my call—
And that isn't all—
He placed my hand in the Master's hand.
Let Him lead you to a better land
To fulfill the purpose in your life.

Though out of the blue, here comes your wife.
Amen.

Thee Vow

Lord, I love thee only.
I don't know why you changed me,
Covered my sins, and rearranged me.
Thank you for the tender touch.
Faith, longsuffering, there's just so much.
To know you is to believe it.
I will receive my inheritance today.
Teach me thee commandment to assure my way
And to commit my life to it.
Pleasing my Lord and Savior,
Unexpectedly receiving favor,
Digging deep until heaven's gates become clear.

Please accept this vow and respond shortly,
Preserving righteousness all for your glory,
Forever near the cross through my heart.

Thank You, Lord, for Bringing Me

Thank You, Lord, for bringing to
The Tree of Life; that's right.

Allowing me to graciously see
All the mysteries of the deepest sea.

Is it Your pleasure
To open unto us Your treasure?

For Your only will is to pay the bill.
Thank goodness I am the patient.

You are the greatest healer alive,
Although the beesting appears real.
Covered in love, we're able to deal.

Time is winding up.
There's just too much in the cup.

Peace Be Still:
It's the Father's Will

There's an End to It All

Ah, how I love his ways
And the long fulfilling days.
He resuscitated my lungs for air,
Somehow changed the atmosphere.
He is wonderful, gentle, and kind.
How perfect for me!
And thoughtful, indeed.
He's marvelous, magnificent, and grandiose.
I hope he's aware of the depth of my love
And how I long to receive help from above.
Ah, how my thoughts are consumed with him.
He's my everything, my all in all, you see.
No one can take the place of thee
For your love is pure.
And I trust him with my life.
Of this one thing I'm sure.
You must meet him.
He and she created them
And all the beautiful trees
With vibrant, colorful leaves.
He made everything right,
Even the gorgeous moonlight.

Thank you for what you've done.
Thank you for a perfect sun.
That shines in the night
And lights up my life.
Thank you for the new start
And for cleansing my heart.
Thank you for the extraordinary places
With friendly and compassionate faces.
O how wonderful his mercy I feel.
He holds my hands and keeps me still.
He fights all my battles, near and far.
O how it thrills my soul
To know that he made me whole.
He is the perfect man,
The only one who understands
All my hurt and grief.
What a great relief
To know that he will always be there,
Helping me to face what I cannot bear.
We know somewhere there's an end.
Wait, the Master can begin again.

Dear Gracious Father,

Thank you for the opportunity to worship the Holy Spirit. How great thou art to let your children return thanksgiving and reverend of someone higher than man. To God be all the glory.

Printed in the United States
by Baker & Taylor Publisher Services